COMPLETELY REVISED AND UPDATED

THE BUSY EDUCATOR'S GUIDE
TO THE WORLD WIDE WEB

Marjan Glavac

NIMA Systems
London, Ontario,
Canada
http://www.glavac.com

NIMA Systems
509 Commissioners Rd., W., Suite 317
LONDON, Ontario, Canada N6J 1Y5
http://www.glavac.com

Discounts of 30% off available for orders of 10 books or more. Other significant discounts are available for educational fundraising, (home and school, student council, fun fairs etc.) business, or promotional use. E-mail **marjan@glavac.com** for more details.

Canadian Cataloguing in Publication Data

Glavac, Marjan, 1955-
    The busy educator's guide to the world wide web

Completely rev. and updated 2nd ed.
Includes bibliographical references and index.
ISBN 0-9683310-1-7

    1. World Wide Web (Information retrieval system).
2. Internet (Computer network) in education. 3. Teaching--
Computer network resources. I. Title

LB1044.87.G59 2000   025.06'37   C00-901111-0

Every reasonable effort has been made to obtain permission for all articles and data used in this book. If errors or omissions have occurred, the author or publisher will update information received in subsequent editions or on the website: **http://www.glavac.com**

Credits

Editor Maria Skale
Cover and Art Kathy Hayes
Otabind Printing Webcom Limited

To Stu Cunningham, a master principal, educator and leader
who taught me all about risk taking,
"pats on the back" and
asking my students everyday before lunch and hometime,
"what did you learn today?"

Read What They Said About Marjan Glavac's
The Busy Educator's Guide To The World Wide Web 1st. Ed.

"Marjan Glavac, a veteran educator and winner of numerous national awards, has created a vital tool in 'The Busy Educator's Guide To The World Wide Web'. His years of successful use of the web and the Internet in the classroom have enabled him to sift through thousands of web resources and document the very best of the best. This guide will prove invaluable to any teacher who uses the web in the classroom."

Caroline McCullen Technology & Learning 1996 National Teacher of the Year
Instructional Technologist SAS Institute, SAS Campus Drive, Cary, NC 27513, USA
MidLink Magazine http://longwood.cs.ucf.edu/~MidLink

"When the students of today graduate into the 21st century, they will arrive into an economy and society that is increasingly wired together - and which is unlike anything that has come before. It is critical that they be provided the outlook, skills, motivation, and awareness that will allow them to make the right decisions with respect to their careers - and indeed, their future. That's why this book can be so useful -- it provides to the teacher some of the background, insight, and resources that can be used to best discover the Internet, and maximize its potential for use within the classroom."

Jim Carroll, C.A. Coauthor of the *Canadian Internet Handbook* www.jimcarroll.com

"I know how busy teachers are and I know how important it is for modern teachers to use the Internet. This book will be of invaluable assistance to busy teachers who need to get on the net."

John Ramsay Former Head of English Centennial S.S. Welland, Ontario, Canada
Author of *Public Lives Private Voices* Oxford University Press of Canada

"This is the book for teachers who want to find engaging Internet resources and activities to use with their students. There is something for everybody!"

Diane Midness, Project Coordinator International School Partnerships through Technology
North Carolina Center for International Understanding
Dmidness@mindspring.com
http://www.mindspring.com/~dmidness   http://www.ga.unc.edu/NCCIU/ispt

"What every teacher needs to know in order to travel the Information Highway."

Edith Jacobson Economics Teacher
Garfield High School, Los Angeles, California, USA

"Includes comprehensive, informative, and easy-to-understand search strategies and techniques."

Kathleen Schrock, MLS author of *Kathy Schrock's Guide for Educators*
http://www.capecod.net/schrockguide/
Technology Coordinator Dennis-Yarmouth Regional School District S.Yarmouth MA, USA

"Be proactive in your teaching. Use the chapters of this book to extend your students' horizons. Let them act locally and think globally."

Bernie Beswick BSc. MEd. Teacher, Loganlea State High School, Australia

"Original and succinct. A wonderful educational tool. The 'Sites That Motivate, Engage And Stimulate Students And Educators' chapter is an excellent reference source, providing a breadth and depth of essential educational information."

David Shaw Junior School Computers Newcastle Grammar School Newcastle NSW Australia

"In the traveling through cyberspace a busy educator needs to find their way quickly and efficiently. Here is your ticket."

Josh Schwartz Summit Middle School
Tech Lab 2000 Instructor Frisco, Colorado, USA

"Educators of the 21st Century need to know the Web inside and out, for their students' sake... and Marjan Glavac shows them every nook and cranny. Cutting through all the Internet hype, this book enlightens users at all experience levels, giving them tools and resources that they can put to use right away. This is one Internet guide that users will want to keep within arm's reach at all times"

Brian Pomeroy Web Coordinator, Children's Hospital of Philadelphia
Author, *"BeginnerNet: A Beginner's Guide to the Internet and World Wide Web"*

"Marjan Glavac has taken the fear out of surfing the Net. You no longer need to feel like a fly caught on the World Wide Web."

Ann Hounsell, Parent, Bonaventure Meadows Public School, London, Ontario, Canada

"A wonderful resource for those teachers who want to catch up with their students!"

Terry Whitmell , John Fraser SS
Mississauga, Ontario, Canada

"In the comparison between our Interstate Highway System and the Information Superhighway on which the Internet is structured, two differences become evident: the Information Superhighway routes keep changing and there are no signposts identifying the exits on the Internet. Well, this book helps with both - it not only helps one navigate the 'where are we now' but also helps one find short-cuts to the 'next helpful web site'."

Earl J. Moniz Librarian Media Coordinator
Lillington Elementary School Librarian, Lillington, North Carolina, USA

"Learning and the Internet are partners for the future. This guide provides a practical view of how to marry technology and learning for high impact."

Elliott Masie The MASIE Center Saratoga Springs, NY, USA (author and technology futurist)

"Being new to the WWW, I find your chapters more than helpful. I am always looking for good sites and not always finding them on my own. Your book seems to be what I am looking for. Thanks."

Carolyn Leyes,
K-6 Computer Aide at Battell School, Mishawaka, IN, USA

"This was a great opportunity - your writing is great and I learned a lot!"

Karen R. Mensinger library-media specialist
Belfair, WA, USA

"A book from someone who walks the talk. Marjan doesn't just talk Internet; he uses the Internet as an integral part of his classroom program. When he recommends sites, or Internet projects, I take the time to check them out."

Louisa Howerow Teacher Librarian, Jeanne Sauve French Immersion Public School
London, Ontario, Canada

"It is similar in format to other books I've seen but it deals primarily with education. Now we won't have to weed through all kinds of stuff to find what is most beneficial to the classroom. It will be a terrific timesaver."

Patricia F. Mayfield Technology Center/Challenge Grant
Lafayette Parish School Board, Lafayette, Louisiana, USA

"In what I reviewed, it looks to me that this book goes a long way to addressing the problem that teachers have in spending excessive amounts of time trying to find useful Internet resources for student learning. The list of educational sites is excellent and the in-depth description of many sites allows teachers to sort through options more easily."

Mike Seymour, M.S. Director Heritage OnLine http://www.hol.edu
CEO, the Heritage Institute Antioch University, Seattle WA, USA

The book seems ideal for those wishing to learn to use the Internet for its intended purpose- the sharing of information i.e. learning and educating. I can see the book being useful for new Internet users of all ages. In fact I will probably give a copy to my newly Internet-enabled parents because it clearly explains basics such as how the Internet works and, more importantly, how to use it in a useful and effective manner. More experienced users, particularly educators or those looking to use the Internet as a tool for finding or sharing information, will benefit from the book's unique focus on education. Although I've used the Internet for 5 years, I learned several things I didn't know including, for example, the details of how searching engines work not to mention the various useful URL's mentioned throughout."

Michael Chachich, Manager, Referential Data Group, Merrill Lynch, Tokyo, Japan

"This book offers a rich resource of information for educators who are looking for those exceptional, award-winning websites. Topical listings of subject areas are included which offer quick access to what you are looking for as well as suggested grade levels and helpful tips for using these websites in your classroom curriculum are included. This book promises to be a great addition to your collection of educational tips for Internet integration."

Tammy Payton First Grade Teacher and Web-Editor for Loogootee Elementary West
Loogootee, Indiana, USA http://www.siec.k12.in.us/~west/west.htm

"Telecommunications can be an extremely effective curriculum tool for both staff and students. Marjan Glavac's first chapter provides a wealth of information for the busy educator looking for great educational sites. Many of the sites mentioned will help teachers realize that technology should serve pedagogy, not the other way around."

Timothy C. Noxel, Teacher Bluewater Board of Education, Ontario, Canada
Osprey Central Public School, Maxwell, Ontario, Canada

"With the plethora of Internet addresses available to educators in books, journals, CD's, and listservs, it's helpful and timesaving to have a collection of websites 'checked-out', organized, and linked to curricular areas."

Roz Goodman, Media Specialist Southwest Region Schools PO Box 90 Dillingham, AK
bsrlg@aurora.alaska.edu

"Trying to juggle your students, keep the administrators happy, and still learn all about the Internet in your spare time? Buy this book, put your feet up, and you'll feel better in the morning."

Jean Armour Polly, http://www.netmom.com/ Author, *The Internet Kids and Family Yellow Pages,* 2nd Edition Osborne McGraw-Hill (June 1997)

"Any teacher who is about to begin teaching the Internet to his/her students, has taught this discipline for some time, or just wants to know which websites benefit teachers the most needs to have this book on or near their desk as a reference guide. Marjan Glavac's concise descriptions of educational websites and his listing of sites by information and services provided is a definite plus over most books of this nature. As an Internet professional who works in a 'computer tutor' environment with all ages of users, I can appreciate Marjan Glavac's use of easily understood language and lack of technical jargon. Although not considered an educator per se, I'll definitely be adding this book to my reference materials collection."

Brian K. Ross Director, Online Content The Komando Corporation www.komando.com

"Amazing, this is one resource book I wouldn't live without. This book makes it possible to pinpoint REAL SUBSTANCE sites without spending the hours, days and months of searching through link after link of sites that sometimes take you absolutely nowhere. Great gift for the teacher, homeschooler or student in your life. I can't wait to explore all these wonderful sites, thanks so much for such a super resource!"

Gayle Remisch, Homeschooler and Canadian Agent for NASA's K-12 Educational Programs - Passport To Knowledge http://quest.arc.nasa.gov London, Ontario, Canada

"There is a never-ending resource of educational information out there and Mr. Glavac has listed some of the very best for any level of education. I've been fortunate enough to visit some of Mr. Glavac's computer classes. I was very pleased to find that each and every student, whether in grade 2 or grade 6, was so entrenched in what they were learning on the WWW that they hardly noticed someone new in the classroom. They were all learning and really enjoying it. I only wish I'd been born 30 years later and had a teacher like Mr. Glavac!"

Cheryl Smelser, Parent, London, Ontario, Canada

"I have been able to be in a few of Mr.Glavac's classes talking to the students about making money on the Internet. (I helped write reviews for web sites for a New York company writing a book called 'NetKids Rule the Net') The students I spoke to were lucky to have Mr. Glavac as a teacher. They were learning on the Internet and they told me how much they liked it."

Nykki-Lynn Smelser, student, London, Ontario, Canada

About The Author

Marjan Glavac (BA, University of Toronto (St. Michael's College); BEd, Brock University, MA, Carleton University) has used computers in education on the first day he began teaching in 1982. Since 1993, he has introduced thousands of students K-University, parents and teachers to the Internet through online courses, websites, classroom lessons, workshops, speeches, articles, his computer columns for *kidsworld* magazine and his latest book, THE BUSY EDUCATOR'S GUIDE TO THE WORLD WIDE WEB 2ND EDITION.

In 1994 he was a recipient of the Roberta Bondar (first Canadian female astronaut)Award for Science and Technology. In 1995 he won the NORTEL National Institute Award for Excellence in Teaching. He was selected to participate in 3 NORTEL summer institutes. In 1996 he won the Prime Minister's Award for Excellence in Teaching Mathematics, Science and Technology. In 1997, he won the Roy C. Hill Award for educational innovation. In 1998, he was awarded a certificate of merit from TVO (Canadian equivalent to PBS.) In 1998, he also wrote his first book, THE BUSY EDUCATOR'S GUIDE TO THE WORLD WIDE WEB 1ST EDITION.

He and his students have been filmed by TVO and Global's Kids TV, featured in all local media-newspapers, TV and radio, nationally in the *Globe and Mail*, *Toronto Star*, *Today's Parent, Home and Educational Computing* and internationally on WGN radio, websites and dozens of student newspapers worldwide.

Marjan has involved his students in projects sponsored by Global SchoolNet Foundation, Kidlink, Academy One, CCCnet, AT&T Japan, Lycos and in the creation of the NewsOntario online newspaper project. K-8 students have also participated in e-mail, travel buddy and research projects with schools all over the world.

He has presented keynotes, workshops and seminars on topics ranging from educational and family software and computer activities to the use of the Internet in the classroom to parents and teachers at international conferences.

His keynote speeches include *Beyond the Rainbow* and *Chalk Board Lessons From The Digital Age* which take the audience on a journey from his first day as a computer fearing teacher to his embracing of "high-tech, high-touch" technology. In a funny and poignant presentation, Marjan shares what inspired him to make his students and school an integral part of the World Wide Web and the Internet.

Marjan is currently a gr. 5 home room teacher at W. Sherwood Fox Public School in London, Ontario, Canada where he resides with his wife Maria and their two children, Vanessa and Collin. He can be contacted by e-mail at **marjan@glavac.com** or through his website at: **http://www.glavac.com**

Foreword

I remember Eric Holden, a brand new middle school teacher, so well. He had been teaching for a month and was totally frustrated in that he wanted suggestions on where to find activities to do in the classroom. The district did not have a new teacher induction program; he did not have a mentor. Basically, he was given a set of textbooks and told to go and teach.

Every new teacher reinvents education all over again. We are a profession entrusted with leaving a legacy for the next generation, yet it is a sad commentary on education that we leave nothing for the next generation of teachers. You would think that a new teacher would be able to find a file full of materials left by past teachers. Instead, we tell new teachers to

Figure it out for yourself,
Do it yourself, and
Keep it to yourself.

I have since heard from Eric and he is doing quite well. What happened? I gave him one or two websites such as:

http://www.new-teacher.com/ (the dash is important)
http://school.discovery.com/schrockguide/index.html

and told him about links. One door opened another, which opened another, and suddenly he had more activities than he knew what to do with.

It took me decades to read magazines and go to conferences before I acquired enough activities for my classroom. Now, with the click of a button, you can find most everything you need.

I still recommend going to conferences and reading certain professional journals. One day I opened "members.aol.com/Jedarling" and found one of the most dignified statements I have ever read on the dignity of teaching. An award-winning English teacher, Judy Darling, wrote two stirring articles

"*To All Outstanding Teachers*" and "*What Good Teachers Know*"

There is a bright future for those educators who are prepared, are positive, and have added value to their lives. In the blink of an educational eye, the power, the culture, and the future of the teaching profession will reside in the new teachers.

I ask you to access **http://www.new-teacher.com/** This is what new teachers are doing. Like the aforementioned Judy Darling, they are creating their own websites and communicating with each other in a very positive manner. The creator of this web site is 29 years old and is typical of the new breed of teachers people who share and chat with each other. They are supporting and helping each other instantly. You can see leadership exuding from these new teachers. They don't need outdated organizations and negative publications. (One journal even sarcastically gives out awards annually called "Rotten Apple Awards" in their endeavor to help teachers become successful teachers!)

The truly good teachers, new or veteran, have youthful outlooks, energy, optimism, immortality, vision, and the willingness to take risks as their common denominator. They are globally, environmentally, and racially aware. Their sharing on the Internet is how they celebrate the success of schools and teachers.

Education is an institution that thrives, succeeds, and grows on hope, help, sharing, love, and caring. We live in an age where synergies, networks, and collaborations will position individuals and organizations to build connections with those who want to provide a better education and life for our students.

I recommend Marjan Glavac's book to all educators. If you dare to teach, you must never cease to learn. Marjan's book makes the learning process so much faster and rewarding. I hope you enjoy his book and learn and grow from it as much as I have.

Harry K. Wong
orderinfo@harrywong.com

Harry K. Wong, who with his wife Rosemary, are the authors of The First Days of School, which has sold over one million copies.

Contents

Introduction

Ever since a student first showed me how to turn on a computer on my very first day of teaching in September 1982, I have been fascinated by the computer. Over the years, I used it as did many of my colleagues, to integrate it with my class curriculum with varying degrees of success. It was just another tool that we teachers used in the class to make things easier for our students to learn.

Then, in 1990 I saw the potential of the computer as a telecommunications tool. In the basement of our house, my wife was working on a 286 Personal Computer with a software program called Telix, connected to a 2400 baud modem and a telephone line. As I peered over her shoulder, I noticed that she was "chatting" in real time to her colleague miles away in another city. I thought to myself that if she can talk to someone, why can't my students?

Three years later, my students had the opportunity to do just that. The Ontario Teachers' Federation were giving Internet e-mail accounts to any teacher for free. The Canadian government was also offering for free, full Internet service to 300 schools across Canada through the SchoolNet initiative. My school was one of those 300.

That year, the walls of my school came tumbling down. My students were involved in a personal poetry telecommunications project headed by two American teachers, Sheldon Smith of California and Robert Fromme of Texas, with schools from 6 U.S. cities; an Art Ecology exchange project with 28 schools in 5 countries (Canada, USA, Russia, Peru and Japan) and a "Day in Life Project" with over 100 schools in 3 countries. Students used the Internet to exchange e-mail with students in Siberia Russia, Israel and South Carolina, USA. One student used the Canadian government computer to interact in natural language for information on AIDS. Another student downloaded information on UFO sightings in Canada and used this information to plot sightings in Ontario for her Science project. Another student played chess every day with my friend in Saskatoon, Saskatchewan, Canada, and beat him. Something I could never do face to face!

When a student from London, Ontario, Canada can read a poem from a student from San Antonio, Texas, USA and shout spontaneously and exclaim "that person is exactly like me", or when a student from San Antonio, Texas can write back and say "I didn't think anyone would write to me", there lies the power of telecommunications-it's the power to connect and network. Many of my students that year found that students in faraway and diverse states such as California, Illinois, Maryland, Texas, South Carolina and in countries such as Russia and Israel, have a lot in common with them. "They're a lot like us", was a phrase often said by my students.

This technology became even more powerful when I noticed the effect it was having on my special education "at risk" students. These students were overcoming their barriers and communicating with peers of their own age without being prejudiced. The technology freed my students from barriers of sexual, racial and cultural stereotyping. They could communicate a message based on the message itself and not on the way they looked, or what they wore or the way they behaved. My "at risk" students were reading and writing letters, something which they would have had much difficulty doing in the past without a computer and without a purpose. They could now begin to overcome their barriers and connect with peers their own age based on their interests.

The technology has since surpassed in a short time what once I thought would take decades to overcome. Computing costs have decreased dramatically over what they were 5 years ago. More and more schools and homes are now connected to the Internet. With the increase in the number of educators on the Internet, there has been an increase in the information available. The increase in information, has brought the challenge of overcoming information overload.

This book is for every parent, teacher, librarian, administrator-anyone who uses the Internet, and more specifically its graphical tool the World Wide Web to teach children ages 4-18 (K-12). It is for anyone who has experienced information overload trying to use the many resources now available on the Internet. It is also for those educators who already have access to the Internet and the World Wide Web and are comfortable and knowledgeable with the basics of navigating the Internet. It is for those educators who have a vision of giving their students the skills they need to communicate beyond the four walls of their classroom to the world and beyond and who want children to read, write, share, build, communicate and contribute using telecommunications. It is for those who want to do all this, in addition to being in the classroom all day with your students, teaching, dealing with discipline problems, collecting fund raising money, providing extracurricular activities, attending meetings, sending home notes, phoning parents and doing all the necessary "stuff" that makes an educator, an educator. You are the "busy educator" in the book's title.

Disclaimer

This book has been written as a resource for educators. However, the publisher and author are not responsible for the material on the pages referenced by these links. The Internet is a wonderful resource, but information constantly changes and sometimes links that have been deemed "safe" for students, are no longer appropriate. Please use your professional judgement and care when allowing students access to these sites. Although all sites have been checked and re-checked, and chosen on the basis of their educational content and relevance to the classroom, the nature of the Internet is such that changes do occur. Some sites may not be appropriate for certain grades, ages and maturity levels. Try to preview the sites, in advance if possible, just as you would preview a video or any other material before using it in your classroom or with your children.

Please be aware that sometimes you may not be able to access all the links in this book. Visitors could be blocked from entering a site because of routine maintenance, a hardware failure, or because of site traffic. Sites can also move to new locations or become discontinued. If you do encounter problems, try to access the site at another time of day or on a different day of the week. Double check addresses for correct spelling and capitalization.

About This Book

Chapter 1 This chapter is designed to get you using the Internet quickly and efficiently. It gives an overview of top educator, parent and kid's sites on the World Wide Web. If your time is limited, this is a great starting point to access excellent sites.

Chapter 2 A number of great sites are listed in this chapter for teachers who want to find more information on educational standards in their own state, other states and provinces, lesson plan sites, theme sites and sites that provide information for teachers, beginning, substitute and experienced at all grade levels.

Chapter 3 The first pages of this chapter contain links to excellent lessons, tips and strategies to integrate the Internet into your class curriculum. The websites in this chapter are classified according to subjects and grade levels. Grade levels are used here as an estimate only, as abilities among schools and districts vary. The following illustrates the approximate ages of students used with the grade categories:

preschool: (Pre-K) ages 0-3; kindergarten: ages 4-6; grade 1: ages 6-7; grade 2: ages 7-8; grade 3: ages 8-9; grade 4: ages 9-10; grade 5: ages 10-11; grade 6: ages 11-12; grade 7: ages 12-13; grade 8: ages 13-14; grade 9: ages 14-15; grade 10: ages 15-16; grade 11: ages 16-17; grade 12 ages 17-18; College and University: 18+ (grade 16).

Chapter 4 There are an amazing number of great telecommunications projects on the Internet and World Wide Web. This chapter looks at some guidelines for becoming involved in a telecommunications project and some things to know before allowing students to go online. Information is also included on where to find projects, how to keep current with new projects and a description of some notable projects which you may want to do with your students.

Chapter 5 A resource is only valuable if you can access it. This chapter shows you some tips on searching for and finding the information that you and your students need and want. In addition to the well known search engines and directories, there is a list of educational sites, and search engines which have been found to be particularly useful for students and teachers. There is also a chart by Debbie Abilock on how to choose a search engine.

Chapter 6 Reg Ferland, my French instructor at Brock University Teacher's College, often gave us "newbie" teachers in training the following advice: "don't reinvent the wheel". With the widespread use of the Internet, there are a lot of teachers who have shared their resources, experiences and expertise with the world wide educational community. This chapter illustrates how you can share your resources with anyone by using your own website, and where you can find additional resources on the Internet to develop and create your own website.

Appendix In the appendix is a directory of all the web addresses listed in the book (except for individual listservs found on the AskERIC site). This appendix is designed to help the busy educator sort through sites and information quickly.

Index The index has been designed again with the busy educator in mind. You will see an emphasis on activities, grades, lessons, and subjects and search tools.

The success of the Internet and the World Wide Web has been based on individuals willing to share and collaborate with others. If you have any favorite sites, projects, tips, strategies, ideas or updates to any sites in this book that you would like to share with others, please e-mail them to me at **marjan@glavac.com** I'll post them in my free newsletter or on our website at:
http://www.glavac.com

Two roads diverged in a wood, and I--
I took the one less traveled by,
And that has made all the difference.

Robert Frost

Chapter 1

How To Use The Internet...Real Fast

"The adjustment to the new contexts is where the work is, not in learning the new technology."

Prof. Jerrold Maddox

What has always attracted me to the Internet has been the dizzying pace of change. Just when I've thought that I've discovered the latest and best educational website, the collective and creative community of the Internet always manages to offer even more and better sites. It is in this ever changing atmosphere that sites which maintain their creativity, offer viewers value for their time and strive to engage their audience in interactive forums and discussion groups, are rewarded by our repeat visits.

I have a rule to determine good educational sites for teachers: will they make my teaching easier or harder? The truly great sites offer teachers help in understanding how to implement this new communications technology into the classroom and developing a curriculum which will prepare kids for the next millennium. It's a challenging goal for many sites which bill themselves as educational. Unfortunately the Internet landscape is dotted with haystacks of educational information and resources. The best sources are as elusive as the proverbial needle. Many of the sites tend to offer links to more links with little or no explanation on the links or how the information can be used in the classroom. The viewer is often confronted with information overload. Great educational sites are few and far between. They vary tremendously. Some fit the neat easy to follow magazine type format of parent and kids sites. Some are subject specific, some are grade specific, some are project specific!

The following sites however, do follow my rule. They have helped make my teaching easier and given my students and others an exciting addition to their curriculum. They tend to inform rather than overwhelm. They are worth the most precious commodity a teacher has...time.

Top Educator Sites

A to Z Teacher Stuff
http://atoZTeacherStuff.com/

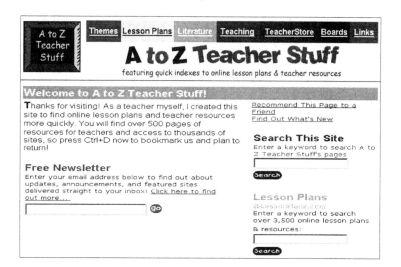

This one-stop resource provides a variety of teaching resources for the online educator. Created by a teacher, it features quick and easy access to thousands of online resources. Find original lesson plans for grades pre-K-12, thematic units and theme resources, teacher tips, educational articles, children's literature activities, top educational sites, and teaching materials. Although the site is extensive, it has a search feature to help you find what you need. Educators can also interact with others on the message boards, or join a collaborative project.

The Theme section is attractively displayed in chart form. Categories featured here include: New Themes and Recent Updates, Seasonal/Holidays, Social Studies, Language Arts/Literature, Science/Health, Math and Misc. Themes. A lot of unique themes here that teachers will really appreciate!

The Lesson Section contains over 175 original lessons submitted by teachers which can be browsed by grade level K-12, new lesson plans, all lesson plans or by lesson plan contributors. A search engine is available to search over 3,500 lesson plans. You can also search them by subject area. Each subject area is further divided into grade categories for easy searching. Teachers won't want to miss the Worksheets and Printable Pages category. Great resources here.

Other sections that teachers would want to check out are the Teaching section featuring A to Z Teacher Tips, and Educational Sites for Teachers.

This is a one stop resource area that you can productively spend your time.

About.com
http://about.com/

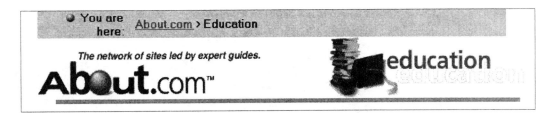

About.com is a vast collection of topic specific sites divided into 28 categories. These categories house over 700 sites. Each site at About.com is consistent in design and function, and led by an About.com Guide. This guide is a dedicated individual who has been hand-picked to provide the best, well-rounded Internet experience in each area of interest.

The education category contains the following subtopics: Adult/Continuing Education, Arts, College/University, History, Languages, Literature, Philosophy/Religion, Primary/Secondary Education, Sciences -- Life/Earth, Sciences --Physical/Computer and Social Sciences.

Currently under the subtopic of Primary/Secondary Education, there are 11 guides offering the following educational sites: Crafts for Kids, Early Childhood Educators, Elementary School Educators, Elementary School Educators: Canada, Homeschooling, Homework Help, Kids' Pen Pals, Math for Kids, Private Schools, Secondary School Educators and Special Education.

The Elementary School Educators site provides educators with the following subjects: Free Lesson Plans, Arts and Crafts, Becoming a Teacher, Classroom Management, Computers/Technical, Departments of Education (US), Early Childhood Education, Finding Freebies, Help for Parents, Homework Helpers, How to Find a Job, How to Substitute, Language Arts, Literature, Mathematics, Multicultural Education, Music and Theater, New Teachers, Physical Education and Health, Science, Social Studies, Special Education, Assessment, Organizations, Books, Educational Games, Geography, Gifted/Talented, Languages and the Millennium.

There are also two other noteworthy sections on this site: the In the Spotlight section highlights an educational Internet site, a seasonal theme and a teacher tool of the week. The Essentials section contains a Teacher Message Board, Free Chalk Talk Newsletter, How To's for Teachers, Hot Education Headlines, Holiday Lesson Plans, Education Chat Room, and Free Lesson Plans. Teacher feedback is encouraged. Bookmark this site and check in once a week.

ACTDEN
http://www.actden.com/

The ACTDEN site is made up of seven DENs or subject categories. Each offers information and interactive features that encourage students to learn and to think:
MathDEN - presents challenging math problems.
WritingDEN - teaches students how to write effectively.
NewsDEN - presents current events in exciting new ways.
GraphicsDEN - introduces students to cool digital art.
SkyDEN- offers a visually stunning introduction to basic astronomy.
InternetDEN - shows teachers how to use Internet Explorer 4.0.
TestDEN - creates personalized study guides for TOEFL (Teaching of English as a Foreign Language) students.

There are a number of features in this site that will appeal to students and teachers. One of the most important is the focus on content by combining traditional methods with interactive ones. Content is presented with both the teacher and student in mind. Student lessons are presented in a very appealing format with graphics used sparingly yet very effectively.

An added feature of this site is the use of computerized online unit multiple choice tests to evaluate student learning of the material. Once completed, the tests are submitted to the ACTDEN computer to be marked. A record is kept of all activity for students through a password system. These quiz tests are aimed at students in grades 7-12.

Log into the ACTDEN and see how online curriculum can supplement your own.

AskEric
(Educational Resources Information Center)
http://ericir.syr.edu

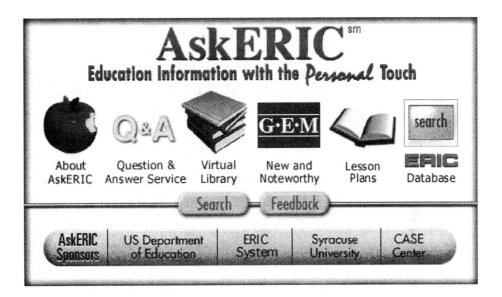

The AskEric website belongs to the Educational Resources Information Center (ERIC) and run by ACCESS ERIC which is sponsored by the U.S. Department of Education, Office of Educational Research and Improvement and administered by the National Library of Education. The ACCESS ERIC site contains the largest education database in the world, with over one million abstracts of documents and journal articles. The place for educational research.

The AskEric site was the first registered education site on the World Wide Web. The Virtual Library link contains more than 1,100 lesson plans, more than 20 listserv archives, 250 AskERIC InfoGuides and the AskERIC Toolbox. There are three main components of this site.

The first for educators and parents is the AskERIC question-answering service. This service is available 24 hours, 7 days a week with a 48 hour response time to answer questions about education.

The second component is the ERIC database This is the world's largest source of education information, containing more than one million abstracts of documents and journal articles on education research and practice. The database is updated monthly, ensuring timely and accurate information.

The third component is the education listserv archive to over 20 educational listservs. A listserv is a mailing list which is targeted to a specific audience.

Some are very technical, others are general. Some are moderated, others unmoderated. Some are very active with over fifty messages a day, others have only a few messages a week. When you subscribe to a list, your name and e-mail is added to the list. You also usually receive a standard welcome letter introducing you to the list and any special instructions unique to the list. From that moment, any e-mail posted to the list by members will be sent to you. You can then read the discussions, send e-mail to individuals on the list or respond to the entire list. This link offers the educator a potpourri of some of the best listservs on the Internet. You don't have to join a particular list to be able to read the messages. Instead, you can browse through the archives available for each one. The beauty of the this AskERIC link to the listserv archives is the incredible time saving feature of the search function. All you have to do is select the listservs you want to search, describe what you are looking for, submit it and voila, specific information ready for you in an instant. Sure beats the old card catalog! Topics on these listservs range from charter schools, early childhood education, and educational technology to middle level education reading, projects, and vocational education. Current listserv archives include the following:

BigSix: Big Six approach to information literacy
http://askeric.org/Virtual/Listserv_Archives/Big6.html

Ecenet-L: Early Childhood Education/young children   (ages 0-8)
http://ericps.crc.uiuc.edu/eece/listserv.html

Edtech: Uses of technology in education for universities and school districts
http://askeric.org/Virtual/Listserv_Archives/EDTECH.html

K12Admin: K-12 School Administrators
http://ericir.syr.edu/Virtual/Listserv_Archives/k12admin-list.html

LM_NET: (Library Media Networking): serving the world- wide school library media community
http://ericir.syr.edu/lm_net/
(This list, co-founded by Michael Eisenberg and Peter Milbury is one of the best librarian mailing lists on the Internet. Every librarian should join this list!)

Middle-L: Middle level education
http://askeric.org/Virtual/Listserv_Archives/MIDDLE-L.html

Projects-L: Project Approach Listserv
http://ericps.crc.uiuc.edu/eece/listserv.html

Canada's SchoolNet
http://www.schoolnet.ca

Canada's SchoolNet is packed with information on Canada as well as information for a world wide audience interested in education. This searchable site has three main categories: SN Today, Learning Resources and Connect and over 20 Program topics on the side panel.

SN Today contains News, Cool Sites, Press Releases, Archives and the SchoolNet Magazine in PDF format. The Learning Resources section presents curriculum and education support materials. There are over 1,000 learning resources here under three categories: Curriculum Areas, General Interest and Federal and Related Institutions. The Curriculum Area contains a wealth of information on the following curriculum subjects: Adult Education, Art, Business Education, Career and Vocational Education, Computer and Information Technology, Entrepreneurship Studies, Family Studies, Health and Wellness, Integrated Subjects and Other, Language Arts, Mathematics, Physical Education, Sciences, Social Sciences, Social Studies and Special Needs Education. Under the Connect category can be found a hyperlist of schools on-line and the best Canadian school sites on the Web and advice for school website builders.

A unique and valuable source of information can be found under the Programs category. There are links to community programs, youth employment services, computers for schools, the SchoolNet News Network program for student journalists, information on First Nations, digital resources on Canadian history and culture. Be sure to check out the Virtual Products section to see the fantastic programs that have been developed for education.

Classroom Connect
http://www.classroom.com/

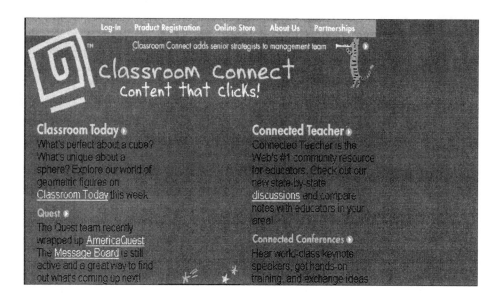

From humble beginnings at a kitchen table in Pennsylvania, this site is the web companion to scribbled notes on a piece of paper that eventually became the Classroom Connect Newsletter.

Classroom Today and the Connected Teacher are two of the main areas of this site. Classroom Today provides Internet links to the curriculum through student activities such as Daily and Weekly Questions, Kids' Quiz, Mystery Media, Survey Says, Connections and other activities. A Topics section provides topics to match curriculum. An Email Newsletter lets you find out more about Classroom Today topics each month. There is also a Teachers' Lounge with planning tools, a teaching guide and tips and ideas on measuring student progress.

The Connected Teacher section of the website links teachers to the latest in state-by-state discussions on education as well as keeping teachers informed on the latest ideas from fellow educators and world class keynoters at Connected Classroom Conferences. There is also an opportunity to read the presenters' handouts and participate in discussions from past conferences. An invaluable addition to any teacher's professional development is the Connected University. There is a free 30 day trial subscription. The following are some of the courses offered: Getting Started On The Internet, My First Web Page, The One Computer Classroom by Tom Snyder Productions, Reading and Language Arts Online, Science and Technology: A Natural Partnership, Teaching To Standards, A Technology Coordinator's Tool Kit, Using The Net To Create Thematic Units.

The once scribbled notes at the kitchen table have journeyed far and wide.

Community Learning Network
http://www.cln.org/

[What's New/CLN Update] [Network Nuggets] [Theme Page Index] [Alphabetical Index] [Navigation Map] [Search Engine]

Welcome to the Community Learning Network WWW home page. CLN is designed to help K-12 teachers integrate technology into their classrooms. We have over 265 menu pages with more than 5,800 annotated links to **free** resources on educational WWW sites -- all organized within an intuitive structure. Since September of 1996, visitors from 165 different countries have made over 16 million hits on the CLN Web site. Thank you and please come again!

The main menu of the Community Learning Network is a well organized source of educational resources for the K-12 teacher. The following links: Educational WWW Resources for K-12 Students and Teachers, Integrate the Internet into the Classroom, Learn More about the Internet, Professional Development in Information Technology and Province of British Columbia's K-12 Educational Community are followed by detailed descriptions and key words. True to its description "CLN provides direct links to exemplary educational WWW resources from our intuitive menus. By finding, previewing, describing, and linking to exemplary sites, CLN's staff save teachers an enormous amount of time that they would have wasted otherwise in fruitless browsing."

The CLN staff also review and update links to resources to eliminate the frustrations of searching for busy educators. Two valuable resources are the daily Network Nuggets and the CLN Update listservs which keep members informed to the latest Internet resources and updates on all the sites that have been added to the CLN site in the past week.

A very useful and fruitful resource for teachers are the CLN theme pages. Here can be found links which focus on a theme found in the K-12 curriculum. The curricular links provide informational resources for those interested in learning more about the topic while the instructional materials links provide support (e.g., lesson plans, instructional tips) for teachers.

The CLN staff have certainly made their site easy to use for the busy educator.

The Copernicus Education Gateway
http://edgate.com

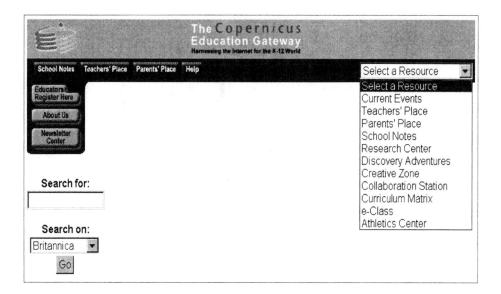

Click on the handy drop down Education Resources menu and quickly go to Current Events, Teachers' Place, Parents' Place, School Notes, Research Center, Discovery Adventures, Creative Zone, Collaboration Station, Curriculum Matrix, e-Class or the Athletics Center. If you need to look up a keyword or subject not found in the Education Resources menu, use the handy search engine. The search engine allows you to search the Copernicus site, the Encyclopedia Britannica and the Internet.

One key feature found here for teachers is the Curriculum Matrix. This very useful feature allows teachers to choose a subject: Science, Mathematics, Arts & Music, Health & Fitness, History, Communication, Reading, Civics, Economics, Geography and Writing and specify a grade from K-12. Clicking on Go takes you to an area of online learning resources, lesson plans and activities all linked to essential academic standards. This is a great starting point for any teacher doing unit and lesson planning. This feature also allows teachers to share their lesson plans and resources with other teachers.

If you need more resources for your lesson planning, head over to the Teachers' Place link and read about more curriculum ideas, lesson plans, professional development, grant information, special education and gifted programs. For something different and creative, click on the Creative Zone. You and your students will certainly enjoy the many wonderful and creative ideas available from the world's best Art museums, Creative Writing, Dance, Music, Theater and Filmaking sites. This is one site that should be bookmarked and visited often.

DiscoverySchool.com
http://www.discoveryschool.com/

As web companion to the very popular television show Discovery Channel , this website lives up to its slogan "The Thrill of Discovery in Your Classroom!" Resources for grades K-12 are easily available through a search engine which covers major subjects in the curriculum. Eight categories of links offer resources to make classroom teaching easier and fun.

The link to the Puzzlemaker category is by far my favorite destination. This wonderful tool has saved me and many teachers hours of work. It's fun, easy to use and the puzzles are a hit with students. There are word searches, word searches with hidden messages, computer generated mazes, criss-cross puzzles, number blocks, math squares, cryptograms, letter tiles and more!

The On TV category features TV calendars for The Learning Channel Elementary School programs for grades K-6 and the Discovery Program Assignment Discovery programs for grades 7-12. There is additional information on the TV shows and links to lesson plans. Another link gives information to teachers on upcoming prime time shows on Discovery Networks.

The Lesson Plans category contains lesson plans for grades K-12. You can see all the lesson plans on one page or just lessons for grades K-6 or 7-12.

Another great resource found here is Kathy Schrock's Guide for Educators. This well organized site is useful for enhancing curriculum and professional growth. It is updated daily to include the best sites for teaching and learning. There are more than 2,000 web links here!

Education World

http://www.education-world.com/

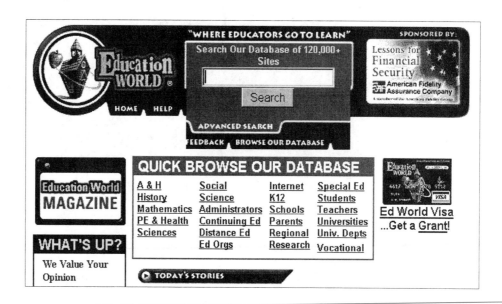

The site "where educators go to learn" boasts a searchable database of over 120,000+ sites! This well laid out site also offers timely information organized into the following topics and subtopics:

Original Content: WHAT'S NEW? Archives, Administrators, Books in Education, Curriculum, Great Sites, Lesson Planning, School Issues, Site Reviews, Special Themes, Teacher Lessons and Tech In Classroom.

Subject Centers: The Arts, Foreign Language, History, Language/Literature, Math, Physical Education/Health, Science, Social Sciences and Technology.

Communities: Counseling, Early Childhood Education, Higher Education, Parents, Preservice Education, Projects, Special Education, Students, Vocational Education.

Feature Areas: Best Of Series, Cool Schools, Education Standards, Employment Listings, Events Calendar, Grants Center, Holidays Center, Message Boards, News For Schools, Professional Development, Research Center, World Resources, World School Directory.

Support: FAQ (Frequently Asked Questions), About Us, Contact Us, Add A Site, Site Guide, Join Mailing Lists.

This site, whose motto "where educators go to learn" is a well deserved one.